SMOKED BLOOD
AND LAVENDER

SMOKED BLOOD
AND LAVENDER

POEMS BY DIANA ELIZONDO

FLOWERSONG BOOKS

DONNA, TX

ISBN 10: 0692411453
ISBN 13: 978-0692411452

FlowerSong Books
4717 N FM 493
Donna, TX 78537
www.flowersongbooks.com

First printed edition: January 2017

Contents

RIPPING A HEART IN TWO

Modern Lilith

No man has made a claim on me
no longer young yet still not tamed
and I intend to stay that way.

Call me a reject, I couldn't care less,
it is I who chooses isolation, not Fate.
I prefer to be a free spirit than a pampered slave.

I'm not condemned nor a mistake,
nor do I make any demands,
I just choose not to have a master.

Although I seem inhuman,
a demon drinking infant blood,
I don't need carnage for sustenance or vengeance.

Unlike the succubus, I hold no grudge,
humans aren't the enemy nor the reason.
I have no use for detours in my path.

I would rather spend my life searching
than have another being offer answers.
Love is substitution for the slothful.

Thus I decline my assigned position
and leave my intended husband to another.

Useless Thing

A heart's purpose is to shatter
In a sadist's sharp, hungry fist,
Ripping a heart in two with a twist,
Then once more to piles of tatter
Dropping pieces that clatter
On the floor, emotional gore.
The body grows cold and sore
Covered with thick stitches and dark scars
Blissful joys will be felt no more,
Eyes dimmed like dusk bleak without stars.

YOUR CAGE

Can't tell if it was love or lust
That pulled me by the neck
When you dragged me with your leash.
Your hunger brought great thrills and fears,
Turning my needs to eternal flames
As I whimpered for more, inside your cage.

I used to kneel when you breathed down my neck,
I used to crawl whenever you pulled that leash,
I used to enjoy how your lies soothed the flames
And pain that would fill anyone with deep fears.
I used to feel content when you locked me in your cage,
Blissful lust.

I once believed pleasure existed in flames
And love lived itself in the bruises on my neck
Whether from your fingers or from your leash.
Your kind words helped me forget common fears
And my humanity when enslaved by sessions of lust.
My will was gone when I was placed in your cage.

Deceived by your gestures and acts of lust,
I grew convinced I was addicted to your flames,
Punishments and strangulations from your leash.
I believed my home was inside your cage
Where I was protected from reality and fears.
Submission rewarded with jewels around my neck.

But I finally see the bars of your cage,
Finally feel the aches carved into my neck,
And see the ugliness behind your caresses and lust.
I became less than human because of your leash,
As my skin turned to ash because of your flames.
Now my arousal is reduced to real fears.

Pleasure can't distract me from my imprisonment in your cage.
Your sadism can't be hidden anymore by divine lust
And caresses no longer soothe scars inflicted by flames.
Can't ignore your teeth stained from kissing my neck
All along, you were the source of my fears.
I never again want to be held by your leash.

Not fooled by the diamonds encrusted on your leash,
Nor the velvet cushioning inside the cage,
I won't go back, burning in those flames.

HER INFERNAL PROSE

Was it depraved having his eyes look up at me? Different position, but still impaled with his heat. It is to Adam, who pointed at the flower bed.

Lie back down, he ordered, but I disobeyed. I kicked his loins repeatedly before leaving him in unfulfilled agony. First man denied by me.

I exited the so-called paradise, searching for home beyond divine borders. The other land is not approved in His image, but is luxurious for a damned queen. My domain to rule, not serve.

Thriving in carnal joys and pleasures, I receive gifts from numerous lovers. All beneath me, satisfied every night.

I'm erased from scriptures, but recalled for female rebellion. Freedom makes the woman more human, not less.

Echoed for Years

Your voice echoed for years
That once brought great contentment
To my mind,
But hearing you now brings fears.
To my mind, your voice echoed for years.
Seeing you caused joyful tears,
Now your absence makes them signs of torment.
Your voice echoed for years
That no longer brings contentment
To my mind.

A Sort of Gratitude

I'm left with mementos of tragedy
On my skin, all black violets.
I've grown tired of being your conquest
With every bit you've taken from my flesh.

I was drowning in my own dark waters
While fading away from the inflictions
That filled my bruised lungs.

Finally tossing the rusty chain and deluded loyalty,
I'll never wish you well nor acknowledge you again,
Though I might reminisce about the moments of naïve bliss
Conjured by your masking charms and fibs.

After all, I'm grateful for what I learned
From years of your hellish sessions.
Love is a word used for traps
And I'm carrying this heavy lesson,
With a grudge and bitterness,
But thank you nonetheless.

I Hate You, I Want You

I
Hate
Your
Ignorance,
Arrogance,
Nonsense,
Lack of conscience,
And masses of madness.
But
I
Want
You
To
Moan,
Groan,
      Shriek,
      Scream,
      Bleed,
      Plead,
      And beg
For
Bliss
A kiss,
More,
      Mourn,
      Whine,
      Cry

For
     Relief,
     And mercy.
I
Hate
You
But,
I
Want
You.

CLAIMED

Trapped in velvet spreads and hovering shade,
Your resistance has been drowned in sealed lips,
As logic fades while every fabric's torn to strips.
Your pleasure's denied by years of learned shame.

Your pride is swept away by each caress,
Your free will broken from sensual stress,
Our fingers entwine as mad lust rears,
And need grows and shows in strained tears.

Now fulfilled into a form of glory.
Your loss has become our victory.

Rose

She's a model of natural beauty
With small petals of soft, apple red
And formed by a wise, caring mother.

She's snatched away by your ravenous hands
that cut and trim for sensual use.
You abandoned her to display her shame.

Don't "dear" me and offer such mockery.
Processed honeyed words won't grant you access
And I reject your poetic lies with flowery fragrance.

A hunter presenting broken trophies,
Your primal intentions hide behind those roses.

A bouquet of your many victims
And I'll never be added to them.

THE WAY YOU LOVE ME

You showed love through orders
To keep me in your arms
And bound by your ring.
You loved that I cried for joy,
You said I looked lovely with tears.
You loved me when you were satisfied,
But hated me when you were not.
You loved how I crawled and begged
Even when you were not aroused.
Crying, begging, submitting
And dissatisfaction brought
Nothing but purple tattoos.

THAT EMPTY PROMISE

Giving me a thousand roses
Doesn't help me forget
They will wither away.

Offering me real diamonds
Doesn't convince me
They will shimmer forever.

Feeding me the best chocolates
Doesn't assure me
Our moments are always sweet.

Telling me you love me
Doesn't stop me from
Counting the times you don't.

ALWAYS

You said "always" whenever you vowed
To me like you meant it.
You added "always" to your
Delivered gifts to be convincing.
When I hear you say "always,"
You're only speaking in bluff.
You claimed we'd always be whole
With arrogance in a bouquet.
Your "always" is never close
To the truth or to your heart.
Your "always" is a false dedication
I'll never believe and accept.

CLOAKED IN MORBID ATTIRE

THE GRACKLE

Like Snow White's stepmother, its eyes are shaded in jealousy. Bright green eyes can't inflict fear like the ones in soulless brown. All black, but small, slim and lame, the grackle can't terrify or inspire like the raven from up north. The grackle makes cracked whistles instead of echoed caws, signaling grim times ahead. The grackle prefers searching for scraps of bread and fried bits of chicken since it lacks taste for decomposing organs. A scavenging nuisance is not suited for the role of a psychic undertaker.

Nightly Theatre

Owls scream, cries echo
Reenactments of murder—
Scenes rehearsed each night.

DEATH IN WILT

Pink rose once divine,
but time has drained her petals
now wilted and gone.

Autumn

Summer's sobbing heavy tears. The heat banished from the earth by chilling breeze howling in triumph. Leaves painted brown and red fall to their deaths at a graceful pace unveiling large hands piercing out like the living dead. Pumpkins sold to sadists as the latest sacrifices: insides ripped out, scarred and burned. Corpses displayed on porches, warding off spirits.

Joys of life fade throughout the land, nostalgia and departed visitors rise from graves, showering the living with senses of awe and dread. Amusing screams and iconic boogeymen plague mortal memories; the bewitching season will soon arrive. Darkness shrouds early across the sky. The moment of worship draws near.

.

Jack O'Lanterns

Pumpkins aren't convenient enough these days
No damned spirit would fear a wee flicker.
Banishing ghosts requires greater craftsmanship.

A bottle grenade flung inside
Glass eyes and wide mouth lighten by ember.
A quick procedure for making wooden faces shine.

There are other hollow canvases needing to be filled.
True beauty comes from orange and red blaze.
Such masterpieces created once a year.

Every sidewalk decorated with giant bright smiles.

THE MOON ABANDONED US

The moon abandoned the suburbs, leaving us with our fears. The moon doesn't look over his shoulders when the light barely illuminates the long roads and street corners while small eyes shine from the darkest distance. The moon hides his disdain, a powdered face that ignores our cries when the creaks and cat hisses echo at midnight and the wind claws and crawls across every roof. Worn out by disappointments and our thanklessness, the moon lets chaos conquer the night when he fades away, leaving us to drown in the dark.

Rain

Secluded, lovely and cloaked in morbid attire,
your presence refreshes me from daily dullness
and the merciless sun's whippings that sting my skin.
You bring soothing gray to cover the faded blue,
and your calls possess such godly authority,
luring me to run out to your embrace.
Though you rarely visit these dry plains,
seeing you through my window in your dark coat
is always a pleasure I savor.
I'm willing to let you subdue me
As you leave me soaked and satisfied.

Noᴠᴇᴍʙᴇʀ

A month-long withdrawal
Between eves of October and December.
Darkness flees yet death remains,
Orange tears have fallen to the earth
And the air is freezing, but still no bleach
To whiten all the surroundings.
The fears gone and the cheers still absent.

Mysticism lingers around us,
But we can't identify its source.
November removed the shrouds of horrors,
And is still bare of winter robes.
When stripped away from orange and black,
November's naked without the green and red.
Just a moment of eerie nothingness.

Outside My Window

The trees creak and crack
As their bare branches bend
And wave with wind's wrath.
Blackness spreads all over
The skies, hiding the viewers
Though their eyes still shine above.
Howls and hisses echo
Across the darkened fields.
The beasts lurk there,
Hiding in the darkness.

THE RIVER

The river reflects
The moon's glow
As the whiteness floats
On the ripples and flow.
The light against the water,
A strong diversion from
The darkness surrounding it,
Hides secrets within.
The river's black waters
Keep broken bottles
And shattered skeletons
From curious eyes
And keep the secrets
That people drown.

DARKNESS IS MY REFLECTION

Maria

Making tamales every Christmas
Until nicotine finally broke her.
Always seen with a scowl
Now replaced with a sad smile.
Distant and stern
I met her at church, one last time.
Thought I knew how to cope,
Was proven wrong before her,
When I choked on my goodbyes.
Knew nothing about my grandmother
Until I found the photos she left behind.
Until my parents told me,
I didn't know her frail appearance
Hid a knife wielder willing to defend
Against robbers and rapists.
She wore crosses around her neck
Now dressed in rosaries and thorns.

WHAT'S HAPPENED SO FAR

Around 1996, I entered middle school where I gained recognition as a Fonzie impersonator thanks to my black leather blazer.

Around 1998, I don't recall anything interesting happening that year. Whatever it was, it wasn't important anyway.

Around 1999, we celebrated New Year's Eve and the world didn't end. I thought it did the second the power went out, but the panicking under my sheets only lasted two minutes.

Around 2001, I saw the world change from a sophomore English classroom as the planes crashed on the TV screen.

Around 2003, after years witnessing the chaos of my parents' marriage, I told my mother being single and childless is easier.

Around 2008, I was in New York when I let some Tibetan monks exit through the door first. Hopefully, I earned extra karma points.

Around 2010, my family and I went to Hawaii where my brother spent the entire vacation earning a reputation as a broken-legged, screaming drunk. You might find him on YouTube.

Around 2013, my brother told my parents that he was going to be a dad. I'm no longer pressed to carry on the legacy.

I Have Lived There all My Life and Should Have Left Long Ago but Couldn't

I have lived there all my life and should have left long ago but couldn't. Native of neither country, I was born shackled by roots buried deep in the ground and too heavy to pull out. Not enough air to scream or whine, but sufficient to keep me breathing.

Time stops for the Valley, but not for us. Buildings multiply and the people keep aging, but the dying green and brown is eternal. Still I would rather die from boredom than the frostbite of the harsh winters roaming the North. I hate having been born in isolation, but I hate conforming even more. Dreamt to fly yet scared to crash. Non-Christians are damned for never hoping for better bliss. I'm trapped in a limbo between two countries: neither can help me escape.

Gothic Nature

Outsiders dwell on dark street corners and explore midnight.
They're not obliged to do so, but it's a sound activity for
    insomniacs.
The demons of materialism and hypocrisy blind the outcasts from
    seeing
the line between rebellion and conformity,

expressing themselves in black attire for attention and pride.
Difference comes from within, not from pale powder,
dark lipstick, boots in spiked armor.

Goths heed the notion of Death as they ponder
And wonder where the dead travel after burial.
They embrace Darkness from inside and out.

Society's fear-filled ignorance sends the Goths into exclusion,
not their need for recognition and worth.
A Goth knows that changes never cease in the shadows,
when keeping the rebel alive despite cultural decay.

THE SHADOWY THING

There's a black figure in front of me
It moves as I do and has my shape.
The figure is like me because it is me.
Darkness is my reflection, my true form—
Always been that way.

That's what I am.

I'm neither Venus nor Adonis,
My face has no features to attract the sexes
Nor do I have a voice to lure them into my arms.
I am only a void with nothing to prove
Having no rights to give or receive.

Not he or she.

Where is the ring to slip onto a lover's index?
Where is the key to unlock the sacred chest?
Where is Medusa's head to petrify the men?
Where is the sword to slay the dragon?
Where have they been hiding all this time?

Nothing below.

I have none of those tools for being admired
A thing that lacks only arouses fear and paranoia,
A black sheet which can't be drawn or colored on.

A shadowy thing.

It's Past 3:00 a.m.

I'm still staring at the ceiling. Conscious, anxious, and nervous from waiting throughout another night, laying on velvet sheets. Thoughts tearing, ripping and clawing the layers of my brain tissue, keeping me awake within the darkness. There's no one to push, punish or pulverize me out of reality and pull me down the pit of temporal death. I saw the black nails clinging to the bed's edge along with eyes glaring red, shining dread: my eyes aren't shut tight. Weariness bringing illusions to life. Overwhelmed with fatigue, I open my drawer and pull out a gun.

To the Wasted King

Bow down and be praised by
the mad man with the paper crown
who gulps nectar with deluded pride.
A twelve-inch needle compared to a mere thorn,
he still blames the world for his flaws.

The king drinks and boasts,
pretending to be Dionysus,
all god-like drunkenness without grace or immortality.
Oblivious to the ridicule and disgust from all.

Blindly living in luxurious shit,
he crawls across the puddle of foul nectar.
Beelzebub incarnate gloats through mumbled buzz.
All is a joke to him as he is a joke to all.
I doubt he'll ever figure it out.

All hail the wasted king
of false pride and wasteful gluttony.

Filled with Ashes

The ashes are too heavy
To carry inside me
As they fill my lungs,
Darken my heart
And clutter my skull.

After the spark fades
The ashes gather and grow
To overload my organs
Leaving me still and numb,
Struggling to breathe.

The spark always returns
Out of the ashes
And burns the weight away
As I stand on my feet again,
But the light never lasts.

The light dies and leaves
Ashes behind to fester once more,
Reducing me back to a doll
Stuffed with cinder and bones.

BLEACHED BLOOD

I never received unfair afflictions.
My parents crossed the bridge without a scratch.
My mother didn't run for me to be born on American soil.
I was taught to speak English without having my tongue shaved
    clean.

My feet only faced hardships on tiles of malls and parks.
Armored well in Great Grandfather's European blood,
I'm always in white camouflage to avoid false accusations and
    gunshots.
The suit gets heavier with the growing guilt.

I only sympathized, but never experienced the indignities that
    burn souls,
I'm annoyed, never torn by the blinded scale that favors
    prejudice.
I obsess over Death without offering meals to my deceased loved
    ones,
no one in my family ever has,
and my native language is reduced to second when my tongue is
    half-formed.

I never experienced having nothing to gain,
being shunned for walking bravely on broken glass,
or facing stones for the sin of struggling to survive.
I can never be like you.

Dreams without Sleep

Lying down with eyes closed
But still awake and thinking
Of dreams I should have.
Instead of seeing exotic realms,
I hear the wind creaking
Inside the walls.
I waste nighttime doing nothing
But waiting to grow tired.
My eyes move behind the lids
As my mind burns with thoughts.
Another nightmare I must endure.

LiMB☺

    I spent four years going from classroom to classroom without being bothered or harassed by my peers. I moved, talked and acted like them, but they didn't see me as one of them. They never tried to get rid of me; my presence didn't bother them much. They never hated me, but they never acknowledged me, either. I was rarely noticed as I passed through crowded halls. When I dropped something, they looked at the fallen pencil and wondered how it had happened. The few who did see me were either startled or frightened.

In Iron

I learned to accept the cold
pressed against my skin,
locked in a cell.
My fingers bloodied
and sore from scratching
the walls.
The moments of warmth
forgotten from days
trapped in freezing iron.
I can't keep myself
from going back inside.

A COUNTRY OF GRAVES

NEVER ENDING

The guns and bombs fire
while cherubs cry
in metallic agony.
People trapped, motionless,
from feasting on pills
and venomous sessions.
Nothing ceases
or changes.
everything keeps descending,
never ending.

THE CIRCUS

Tonight is the circus's final night,
spectacle of odd charades and atrocities
of fire starters, psycho gunners, whorish clowns
and chimps in suits that sling mud at one another.

The clowns bow after their lackluster stunts,
the crowd laughs at the oblivious jesters
with fake smiles stretching across smeared makeup.

The other actors burn and shoot everything they can find,
shouting at the audience to look at them.
The people frown, but are still entertained.
The performers exit the stage
leaving blood, ashes and filth behind.

The ringmaster realizes the exploitation has to end.
The crowd saw every gruesome act from the troubled performers
and senseless tricks from the lethargic harlequins.
They will grow tired of the endless encores.

The tent goes down and the show is finally done.
The freaks are gone along with the clowns,
Leaving a barren field, littered with faded posters.

VAMPIRE KINGDOM

They hold our existence in sickly pale hands
Never spare the weakest of society
Predators in suits and deceiving smiles.

Draining our essence 'til we cease living
Stripping our rights; reduced to livestock
As they consume their bounty with bloody greed.

Spitting lies at their prey from both sides
No monster exempt from centuries of infliction
Your dedication's worthless to infernal gluttons.

Dwelling in white palaces, staring down with hungry glares
Mindless, broken mortals prepared for endless feasting.
Lugosi's corpse rolling in shame.

Human herd, too deceived and dumb to revolt
Undead worshipped and guarded under the sign of freedom
A monument of a stake, such atrocious irony.

Ill-fated mortals produced, never born
In the kingdom of vampires.

THERAPY

Poisoning minds to rid ailments,
healers hide ignorance behind coats and degrees
while their prescriptions mask sadistic apathy.
Reckless treatments paralyze chatty lunatics
into breathing bodies robbed of souls.

Protecting the sane by entrapping the abnormal in cushions
and contagious madness doubled in strength
by powerful paranoia and superstition.
Cries echoing through halls mistaken for crazed fury,
suffering ignored like the damned.

From manic to withdrawn,
zombies made through pills, replacing volts.
Voodoo civilized.

Driving through Spotlights

Night sky stripped of moon and stars, replaced by gray clouds. The buildings vanished from my view, leaving a long road shined upon by street lamps, a frozen, black river up ahead. Realized that I ventured too far from the city, decided to head back. I took a left and found a long, barren road with street lamps placed on each side replicating an image of a hallway in a gothic manor. Even with Katy Perry on radio, nothing distracted me from the unsettling feeling of isolation, wishing for other cars to drive by.

Looking ahead, a group of small figures under the spotlight of a street lamp. I drove closer and saw children standing in a circle laughing at a girl with her mouth wide open and cheeks reddened and wet, clenching her stained skirt on her knees in a red puddle. I drove on and looked ahead, turning the volume up.

I heard a loud bang to my right: my eyes turned to see a man lying in another spotlight. There were people walking across, unaware of the dead body on the ground, the bloody footprints left behind. I kept driving, looking ahead, and turned the volume up some more.

Further down the road, slammed the brakes when my path was blocked by white men in business suits furiously stomping on the ground. A mouse running around, tied to a small pole escaping from giant soles. I honked at the men to get off the road, but they kept trying to kill the mouse without even flinching.

"I could just run them over. No one would know," I thought, remembering the children, the people walking by. "One hard step against the pedal, they'll be dead like old dogs."

Overwhelmed by my superego, just drove around. Took a left turn, my apartment complex was up ahead and drove towards the parking lot. Getting out of my car, images still branded in my memory, my hands shook with fear, but mostly by guilt and frustration. I went inside and locked the door. Took my pills before bed.

THEIR REIGN ENDS

Keeping distance for survival, we wait for their deaths with centuries-old disdain. Hiding in holes from above and below, we observe the balding mammals waste their existence, destroying each other and everything else. Destroy to gain and repress to control is their nonsensical notion of life. Manmade pandemonium as blind dedication to their pointy temples, but not God. Annoyed at the brats He made, He is finally pushed to fulfill their careless requests for assisted suicide, leaving the anti-Christ without a purpose.

Climbing out of the ground and the trees, shielded from apocalyptic chaos, our patience pays off as we are freed from our minority status and rebuilt from the remains. Once often tolerated for our squeaks and fluffy tails but mostly called vermin for taking up space in their excluded civilizations, we lived on as we looked out our windows, sockets of ivory skulls, as we claimed the world once more like our ancestors after the dinosaurs. Saluting the extinct species with little fingers aiming at the ground.

FOOD CHAIN

The rats ate the pigs as they lay without care
And they ate the crickets that won't stop chirping.
The dogs were devoured, ending their nightly howls.
No animal is spared from the rats' sinful hunger.

The rats feasted on donkeys and rabbits too,
Even the cats were eaten in one gulp.
Disease spread by their eternal gluttony.

The rats will eat without fearing poison,
Traps, guns or other threats from the people
Who fear being consumed and left headless.

The rats are slowly eating the flag,
Gnawing away the green and white,
Leaving the bleeding eagle behind.

THEY ARE COMING

We're chased in burning wastelands,
Forced to hide in cars and vans,
And barricade ourselves in torn shacks.

What we do won't matter
They are coming.

Swarms searching through cities
They reaped hundreds away, but look for more.
They're always hungry, always hunting.

They are coming.

To them, our survival is illegal
We can't live there or even here.
We're not allowed to be human.
Both sides are infested with monsters.

They are coming.

Our home becomes a country of graves
And the free lands are a lie they created
To lure and trap us in endless despair.

We see each other as abominations
And say, they are coming.

LA LLORONA

She looks for the children
Who vanished in the river,
Leaving their mother wandering
Every night to search in vain
For the right amount to help her back
Into their small arms again.

A ghost of hopelessness and heartache,
She'll never find happiness
When she can't cross back to her home
To unite with her loved ones.
Her children only see her in their memories.

A mother without children
Is a curse for the dead.

EMPIRE

Sight will be regained in stitches,
The thick smog will clear,
And the cords will be unplugged.
The empire will burn in mortal hands
When all nine infernal circles rise.

THE BLACK DOGS

The black dogs run and pant to survive
The bullets and saws.
They travel in packs, but leave some
With broken paws or dried throats behind.
No hope back home and hardships lurk out here.

The mutts can also swim across waters
Said the armed hogs guarding the fence.
They charge, trample and tear up skin
To keep black dogs from bringing the Armageddon
That foams in each of their mouths.

The dogs howl baritone prayers in hot nights
And look around to see if anyone notices,
But no one cares to answer their cries,
Except coyotes who promise freedom
And guide them to slavery instead.

The black dogs continue running and panting
To survive the horrors from both lands
The bullets and saws.

THE MODERN WEST

The showdowns and gun smoke
Have returned as this year's trend
As everyone buys pistols
And wears them with confidence.

Disputes over parking spaces resolved
With a body bleeding through its holes,
And paranoia fueling the urge to pull
Triggers and kill anyone within a few feet.

Justice placed in our hands as we grow mad
With constitutional rights and invincibility
As we state protection to disguise
Manslaughter and trivial squabbles.

We gain warmth from holding guns,
While shooting at our enemies
With burning relentlessness and pride.
We put *Blood Meridian* to deep shame.

SCREAMING HEADS OF CLAY

JOURNEYS

Overwhelmed by boredom again, I left my bed to venture out of my house. I went out prepared with my mouth sewn shut to keep pig demons from bleaching my tongue and wearing sneakers to run from Cerberus whose eyes flash red and blue. In travels, I encountered plastic, vain dolls with necks stretched up to the clouds who wanted to remold me to their unoriginality. Whether running or soaring to the skies, I never feel the wind against my face, but instead a presence embracing from behind. All the while searching for the river princess to get me across to the other side and slay malicious seraphs that breathe endless lies. I returned home, still tired and gaining nothing.

BEFORE I PAINT

My latest model has finally arrived. No appointments made, as usual in these cases. Walking up the stairway, he came into light, letting me examine him from distance. Young adult in early twenties, hair shoulder long and shining gold. Quite built, but not too muscular.

He entered my office and poured himself some wine. Without my permission of course, though never bothered by that manner. After finishing his wine, the model took a few steps, slow, clumsy and shaky. I grabbed his shoulders to hold him still. Refusing my aid, he struggled out of my hands. He pushed me away, his foot slipped, fell down the stairs.

I watched him tumbling to the tiled floor, hearing bones crack like marionette limbs. Following down the stairway, eyes still locked on him staring back at me. Looked more divine on flowing crimson beneath than white marble alone. I captured his beauty with a flash of my camera, anxious to begin painting.

Iron Dragons

I watch the iron dragons guard the dry red sands,
While sitting on piles of velvet bones, listening to
    medicine
As visions of love and vengeful dead enter my skull.

The dragons let the sand pour into the glass.

I witness alternate themes of the apocalypse,
Supernovas, terror missiles, and merciless storms
Blowing man right off of the earth.

The sands continue to fall.

I drown in confusion and ecstasy,
And give my loving demon a ghostly smile
As it feeds me blood flavored kisses.

The crimson sands are almost gone.

I spend the remains of the wasted night
Sipping yellow eye tea, while conjuring tremors
And carving grins on screaming heads of clay.

The glass above now empty and the one below now full.

Walking Through

Down the narrow, dim halls where the judge waits,
I paced between walls painted in worn black,
Trying not to disturb the residents passing by
As they glared in yellow and others glanced in red.

They think I am a foreigner with colonizing intentions,
But their suspicions are wasted on me at every step
While I peek through open doors displaying horrors.

A limping centaur freshly skinned for amusement,
Burned corpses bound in chairs and stools,
And pale men with foreheads branded by hot halos.
Nightmares witnessed from every corner of the mind.

I pass the halls and enter the lobby filled with suspects
Gathered in an endless line as they wait for their sentences.
The tail coils itself to decide where the souls should descend.

After years watching the unfortunates walk out or fall,
I went up the staircase leading to the pedestal.
The judge pondered with tapping finger and straightened tail
As he observed my deeds and thoughts through my eyes.

I tried to view the towering entity with seeming courage
As I stood and waited for the tail's position to state my fate.

RED ROOM

A space formed into a square with an exit on each side. Poorly painted with doorframes badly stained, the room is new, though it seems I've been here before. From a film or a childhood dream that was almost forgotten.

In the red room, blank faces with eyes stare at nothingness. Everything including me is ignored. Perhaps I remembered an old wound inflicted on me years ago or I learned some chances aren't worth taking, both in ambition and romance. All coming from an ill-built room in dried blood and dirty magenta.

WOODEN BOX

I quiver from the terror lurking in you
as you sit on the table proudly
taunting me with your secrets.
Mild curiosity mutated into temptation,
I'm seduced to wonder what's inside you, box.

Well carved and smoothed to perfection
beautiful deception fully recognized,
you lure mortals to seek what you hide inside.

Old gems, nostalgic trinkets or Pandora's leftovers,
do you have what I horribly desire or regret?
I'm trapped between caution and recklessness.

My hands ache to touch your apple shine,
rip open the shell to expose your possessions.
My fear of consequences shattered in small shards.

I can't tolerate this irritating madness
As my fingers press against the cold lid.
Vicious eyes and fangs revealed in the opened box.

Lost in Rome

The rain pours and fills the edges of every street and road as I try to find my way out of Rome. Shielded by the ancient arches while surrounded by the endless rows of pillars, I can't find the way out of the city where the skies refuse to remove their gray veils. I wander farther down the alleys, but I'm still surrounded by Rome's towering fangs that threaten to devour me. There is no one around as I walk in the endless showers and feel the Roman disdain following me. Are the people waiting for me to go away so they can walk their own streets again? Am I too foreign to be where I never want to be? Am I so tainted that the rain won't stop washing over me? Rome continues to harass me while I try to leave that damned city. There's no exit and I have to dwell in the infernal rain and empty streets for eternity or until I make the effort to die.

Dying by the Rotting Oak

I saw the world end while dying
By the rotting oak with fading eyes.
I witnessed no explosive light
Or animated nightmare
Smothering land and sky.

No bombs raining from human hands
Not even the ravenous dead forming swarms
As I was dying by the rotting oak.

Everything blackened in minimal climax,
Oblivion spread everywhere like spilled tar
And sounds were silenced by numbing darkness.
No one gasped when they were being swallowed
By the hungry mass of darkness.

Without blinking or reliving past moments,
I felt the sun's warmth slip from my skin
When the growing shadow crawled towards me,
Shrouding the view of the field from my vision
As I was dying by the rotting oak.

The conclusion wasn't glorious or gruesome
It didn't bring pain or a sensual release
And I'm left disappointed in the blackness
After seeing the world end while dying
By the rotting oak with fading eyes.

MOUTHS

They're big,
Small,
Fresh
And foul.
They whisper,
Mutter,
Yell,
And growl.
They spawn
Stories,
Songs,
And fables.
They spread
Wisdom,
Knowledge,
Lies,
And bullshit.
They're silenced
By rubber balls,
Rolled up socks,
And used cloth.
They're broken
By fists,
Stones,
And clubs
Ending stupidities
And protests.

Silence rules everything
When mouths are shut
With stitches of thread.

APOCALYPSE

Apocalypse arrives in a lightning bolt, her footsteps break the earth as lava bleeds from its cracks, dried black and acid rains in gallons from her eyes as she cries out bleached flames.
Desperation drives mortals to rip out their own teeth to purchase immortality and survive the scorching darkness, while idiots try to drive across oceans in pink Cadillacs.

Apocalypse's reign reduces mankind to cattle in an endless stampede, forces dead mothers to spit out fetuses as they lay in their open graves and leaves cities buried in sand. Her merciless glare is known everywhere by the gray floating above us and the echoes of her footsteps.

THE SCREAMING HOUSE

    I seek answers inside a house that screams, "Forgiveness is pointless!" Its voices echo through the halls while I rip a serpent's stomach open and find a tiger inside. Walls crack and fire rises from the floors as my teeth turn to powder. I find a flooded hall and swim my way into a bedroom where lovers once wasted their breaths for small bliss. More voices scream inside the house and I run out of the room to find zombies in the hall. There are no answers inside a house that screams, "Forgiveness is pointless!"

CHATTY SKELETONS

We sit on our head stones,
Eating sweet bread and sugar skulls
That slip through our bones.
Our bare teeth click and clack
When we talk about the bouquets
Brought to us by our loved ones
Who we left behind years ago
Or the children we never met.
We no longer have eyes
But we can still look back
And tell stories about our pasts.
We live like we did before.
We remember, feast and chat.

AUTHOR BIOGRAPHY

DIANA ELIZONDO was born in Laredo and spent most of her life in McAllen, Texas. She earned her Master's degree in English at University of Texas Pan-American and an MFA in Creative Writing at the University of Texas Rio Grande Valley. Diana's poems have been published in literary journals such as *Yellow Chair Review* and anthologies such as *Along the River 2: More Voices from the Rio Grande*.

ACKNOWLEDGMENTS

"Modern Lilith" was published in UTPA's *Gallery* 2012. "Therapy" was published in UTPA's *Gallery* 2015. "They Are Coming" was published in *La Noria* in 2013. "The Circus," "Their Reign Ends," and "That Shadowy Thing" were published in *Along the River 2: More Voices from the Rio Grande* (2012). "Vampire Kingdom," "Jack O' Lanterns," "Driving through Spotlights," and "Before I Paint" were published in *Along the River 3: Dark Voices from the Valley* (2014). "Chatty Skeletons" was published in *Yellow Chair Review* in 2015.

OTHER TITLES FROM
FlowerSong Books &
Juventud Press

transplant

POEMS BY SHIRLEY RICKETT

Transplant
Poems by Shirley Ricket.
ISBN: 978-0692354339
FlowerSong Books

Where is home? Mostly in the mind and spirit. If we visit a place where once we lived, it's the memories crowding in that take us back, not the plaster and brick. Moving is in our DNA, even if we have lived in the same place for years. The wood and glass changes because we change. In The Poetics of Space, Gaston Bachelard says that all inhabited space bears a notion of home, and that an entire past comes to dwell in a new abode. Transplant explores these themes of change and loss, and aging, and more. It seeks to carry out what Bachelard calls the function of poetry: "to give us back the situations of our dreams."

LA ESPIRAL LOCURA DE LA

ALEJANDRO CABADA

La espiral de la locura
Alejandro Cabada
ISBN: 978-0692411520
FlowerSong Books

Quince cuentos de una de las imaginaciones más singulares de la literatura oscura. Una travesía a lo desconocido. Un viaje escalofriante a lo fantástico. Un salto tenebroso al vacío psicodélico de las emociones fuertes. Alejandro Cabada te acompaña al dominio de lo onírico, donde todas las leyes de lo establecido son destruidas y no hay tiempo ni espacio para meditarlo. Abróchate el cinturón. La espiral comienza a girar.

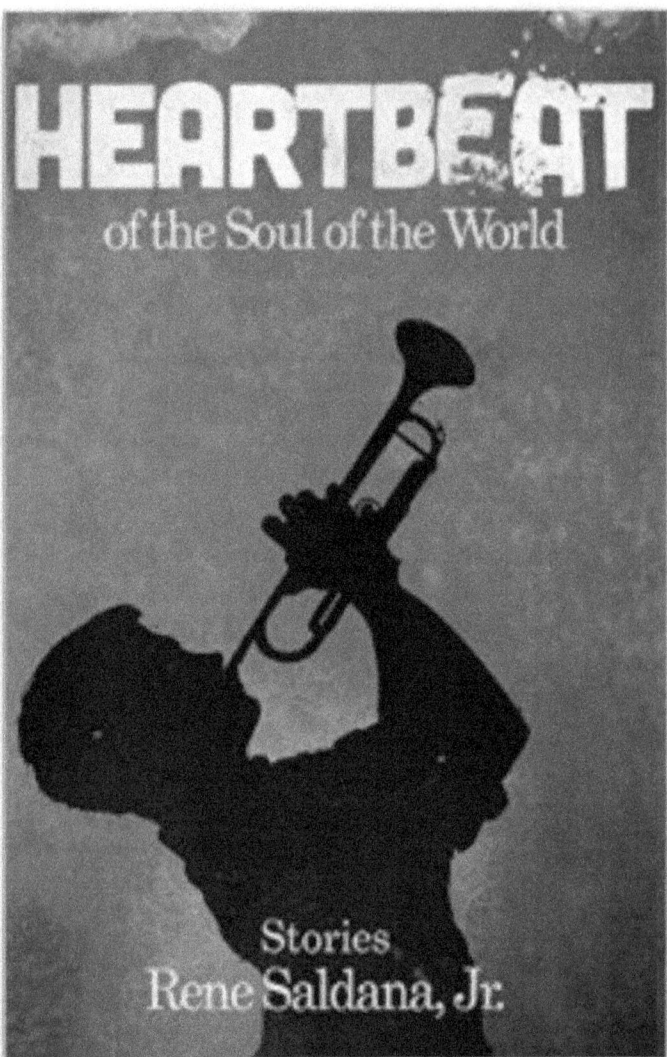

HEARTBEAT
of the Soul of the World

Stories
Rene Saldana, Jr.

Heartbeat of the Soul of the World
Stories by René Saldaña, Jr.
ISBN: 9780692412039
Juventud Press

A young man finds his voice in jazz, leaving a mark on his community that will never be erased. Another discovers his words in books and carves them into angry poems. Bullied kids at the end of their rope are given friendship and protection, while other teens cannot clear the hurdles life sets in their way. And at every step the promise of love glows bright even in the gloom of teenage life. In this new collection, René Saldaña, Jr., echoes the rhythmic pulse of life along the border. These brave, nuanced, accessible stories—ten previously published and five new—will resonate with young readers everywhere, especially Latinos. Come. Lean in close. Listen to the heartbeat of the soul of the world.

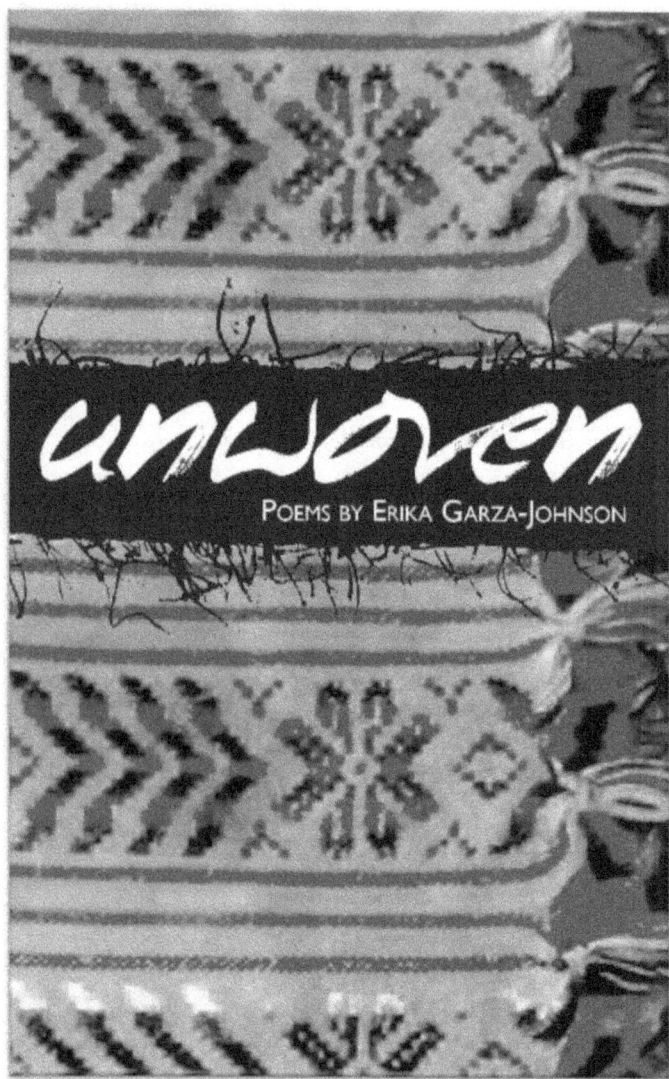

unwoven

POEMS BY ERIKA GARZA-JOHNSON

Unwoven
Poems by Erika Garza-Johnson
ISBN: 9780692323908
FlowerSong Books

The first poetry book from one of the most distinctive voices in South
Texas, *Unwoven* is an unflinchingly honest exploration of Chicana
womanhood along the border, a scattering of quetzal feathers and jade that
celebrate the achingly lovely paradox of life on the edges and in the middle.
Playful, artful, and wholly memorable, these poems prove Erika Garza-
Johnson deserving of her enduring moniker: *La Poeta Power.*

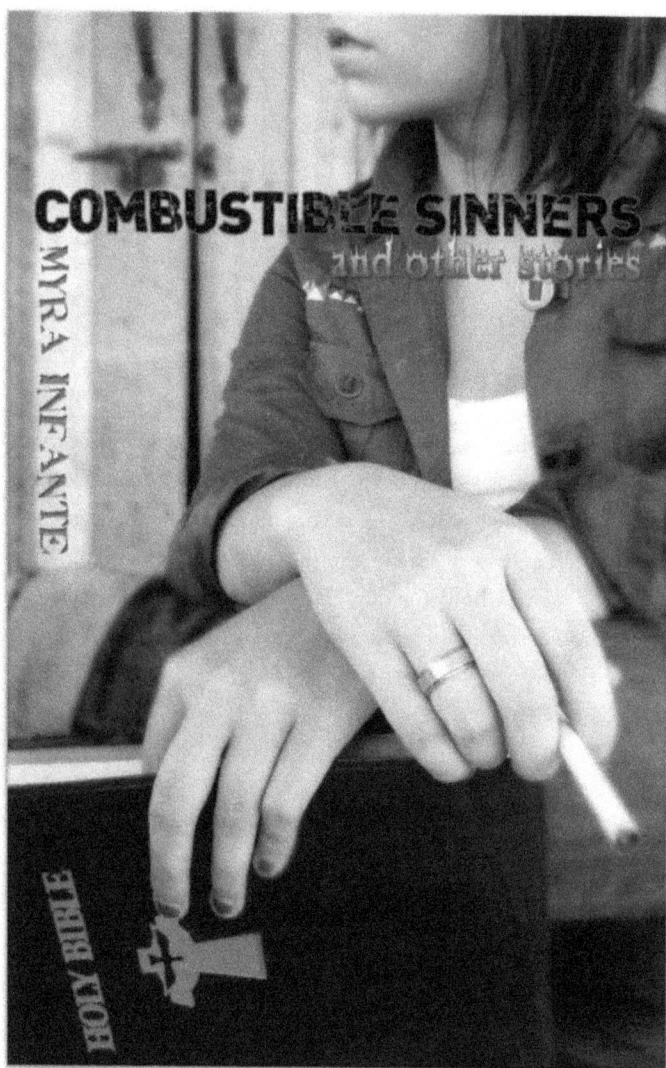

COMBUSTIBLE SINNERS
and other stories

MYRA INFANTE

HOLY BIBLE

Combustible Sinners and Other Stories
by Myra Infante
ISBN: 9780615556703

Lissi Linares is a pastor's daughter whose love for others contrasts with her fear of eternal damnation. Little Jasmine "Jazzy Moon" Luna is determined to save Jesus from being crucified. Naida Cervantes hides a brutal secret behind shapeless, florid dresses. Hermana Gracie tries to set her son up with a good Christian girlfriend, only to make a surprising discovery. Zeke wants a new guitar and Ben wants a cool girlfriend, but what they find as migrant workers in Arkansas changes their desires. These individuals and others try to negotiate the often rocky intersection of faith and culture in seven independent but intertwining tales that explore life in an evangelical Christian, Mexican-American community. Frank, funny and heart-breakingly real, this volume explores themes of identity, culture, religion and sexuality in the context of a little-known subset of Hispanic culture.

¡JUVENTUD!

GROWING UP ON THE BORDER

Stories and poems edited by
René Saldaña, Jr. and
Erika Garza-Johnson

¡Juventud! Growing up on the Border
Edited by René Saldaña, Jr., and Erika Garza-Johnson

ISBN: 9780615778259

Borders are magical places, and growing up on a border, crossing and recrossing that space where this becomes that, creates a very special sort of person, one in whom multiple cultures, languages, identities and truths mingle in powerful ways. In these eight stories and sixteen poems, a wide range of authors explore issues that confront young people along the US-Mexico border, helping their unique voices to be heard and never ignored.

Featuring the work of David Rice, Xavier Garza, Jan Seale, Guadalupe García McCall, Diane Gonzales Bertrand, and many others.

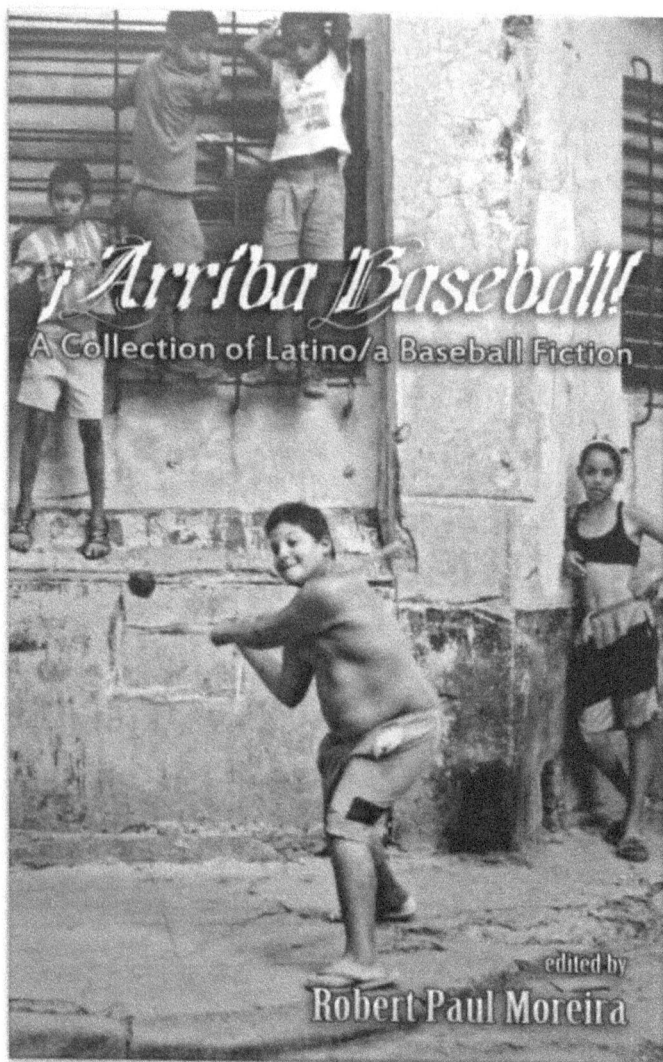

¡Arriba Baseball!
A Collection of Latino/a Baseball Fiction

edited by
Robert Paul Moreira

¡Arriba Baseball! A Collection of Latino/a Baseball Fiction
Edited by Robert Paul Moreira

From Dodger Stadium to the Astrodome, from the Río Grande Valley to
Chicago, from Veracruz to Puerto Rico, from high-school teams to stickball
in the streets, from the lessons of fathers to the excited joy of daughters,
from massive cheering in the stands at Wrigley Field to the dynamics of
family and community echoing on the diamond, these fifteen stories use the
sport of baseball to explore geographical, cultural and dream-like spaces
that transcend traditional notions of the game and transform it into a
universal yet wholly individual experience.

Featuring the work of Dagoberto Gilb, Norma Elia Cantú, Nelson Denis,
Christine Granados, René Saldaña, Jr., and many more.

other titles | 91

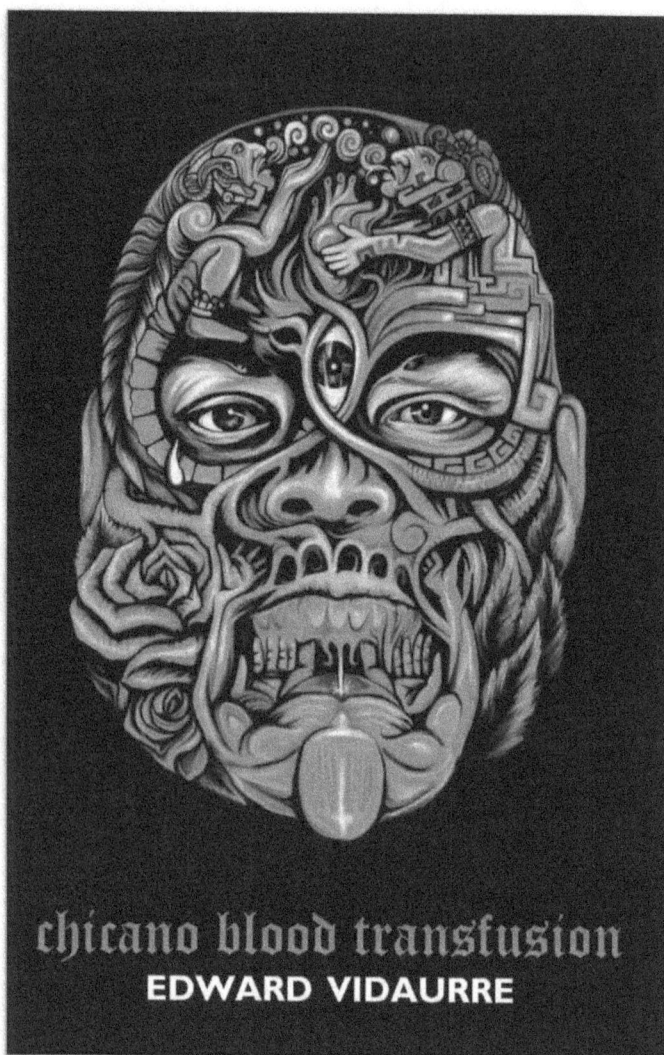

chicano blood transfusion

EDWARD VIDAURRE

Chicano Blood Transfusion
Poems by Edward Vidaurre
ISBN: 9780692411469
FlowerSong Books

Sometimes the grind of life in modern America sucks Latin@s dry: between
the daily micro-aggressions and institutional racism, la gente find
themselves drained of that essential chispa. At times like those, we need a
Chicano blood transfusion like the one Edward Vidaurre injects straight into
our souls in his most recent collection. So just lean back and let yourself be
guided through the graffitied recesses of our collective barrio by one of the
most important poets of deep South Texas, whose unique voice blends
street, Beat, form and striking breadth.

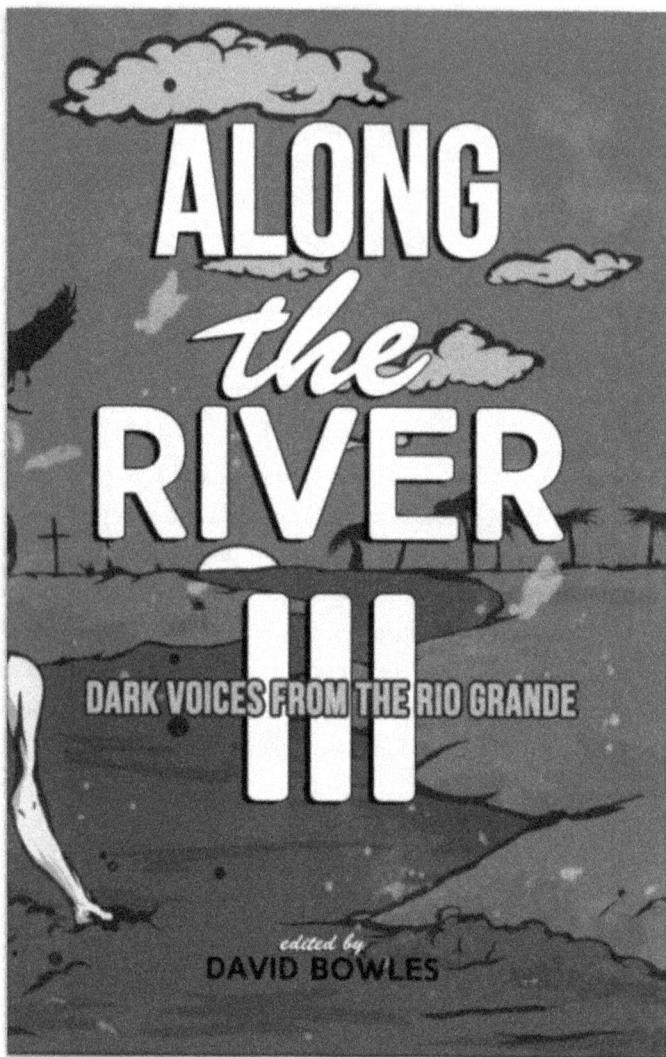

ALONG *the* RIVER III

DARK VOICES FROM THE RIO GRANDE

edited by
DAVID BOWLES

Along the River III: Dark Voices from the Río Grande
Edited by David Bowles
ISBN: 978-0615956183

The third anthology in the *Along the River* series.

When the sun sets on the Río Grande Valley, all manner of dark voices begin to croak, snarl and wail. Come explore the black shadows amidst the mesquite and palm trees down at the water's edge...just have a care not to fall (or be pulled) into the current.

Featuring the short story "Niño" by Álvaro Rodríguez.

FLOWERSONG BOOKS nurtures essential words from the border-lands. The imprint is named for the Nahuatl phrase *in xōchitl in cuīcatl*—literally "the flower, the song," a kenning for "poetry."

Our mission is to promote both the voices of writers in the Río Grande Valley and the literacy of Latinas and Latinos in general. To achieve these goals, we are implementing a multi-tiered strategy:

- editing an annual anthology of local talent (*Along the River* is the name of this series)
- publishing a small number of titles by Valley authors (or by authors whose work would appeal to readers in the Valley) each year
- procuring top-notch authors to edit anthologies of established and upcoming writers whose work has special relevance to the Río Grande Valley
- providing creative writing workshops to aspiring local writers
- conducting writing contests for elementary and secondary children